My Life as an Immigrant

written by Leigh Lewis • art by Alice Larsson

AMICUS ILLUSTRATED
is published by Amicus Learning, an imprint of Amicus
P.O. Box 227, Mankato, MN 56002
www.amicuspublishing.us

Editor: Rebecca Glaser
Series Designer: Kathleen Petelinsek
Book Designer: Emily Dietz

Library of Congress Cataloging-in-Publication Data
Names: Lewis, Leigh author | Larsson, Alice illustrator
Title: My life as an immigrant / Leigh Lewis ; illustrations by Alice Larsson.
Description: Mankato, MN : Amicus Learning, [2026] | Series: My life with... | Includes bibliographical references. | Audience: Ages 6-9 | Audience: Grades 2-3 | Summary: "Paola, an immigrant from El Salvador, shares her experiences of adjusting to life in the US, learning English, and making friends. Paola is real and so are her experiences. Learn about her life as an immigrant in this illustrated narrative nonfiction picture book for elementary students"—Provided by publisher.
Identifiers: LCCN 2025014234 (print) | LCCN 2025014235 (ebook) | ISBN 9798892008853 library binding | ISBN 9798892009515 paperback | ISBN 9798896850175 ebook
Subjects: LCSH: Immigrant children—Social conditions—United States—Juvenile literature | Immigrant children—El Salvador—Juvenile literature
Classification: LCC JV6600 .L49 2026 (print) | LCC JV6600 (ebook) | DDC 305.23086/9120973—dc23/eng/20250707
LC record available at https://lccn.loc.gov/2025014234
LC ebook record available at https://lccn.loc.gov/2025014235

Printed in China

About the Author

Leigh Lewis is a writer who has been lucky enough to have called many places home, including Turkey, Greece, England, Japan, Russia, and her birth country of the United States. Leigh spends her time dreaming up stories for kids of all ages, including her own three—Sanay, Selis, and Tola.

About the Illustrator

Alice Larsson is a London-based illustrator originally from Sweden. A natural creative, she is thrilled to be able to connect characters and stories through her work. Outside of drawing, Alice loves spending time with family and friends, as well as reading books and traveling, which sparks her creativity.

Hi! My name is Paola. I like to draw, read, and play violin. I play soccer and volleyball, too. I was born in El Salvador and I'm an immigrant. I moved to the United States when I was five years old. Let me tell you about my life.

I miss El Salvador, but it was dangerous. There had been a war, then a big earthquake. People were very poor. The US was a safe place to go.

Grandma Lulu came here first. She moved to Ohio. My aunts, uncles, and cousins followed. My mom, my sister Evelyn, and I came last. I was so excited to be reunited with everyone, including my cousin Andrea!

Starting school was scary. I spoke Spanish, and it seemed impossible to learn a second language. Vowels were especially tricky. Mrs. Jones was my English language teacher. She was patient and lots of fun. I learned quickly.

E f g

Now, I go to Mrs. Jones's class as a translator. I help her teach the new kids. I help my little brothers, Gael and Giovanito, learn English, too.

My classmates are from all over—the US, El Salvador, Somalia, Haiti, Venezuela, Honduras, Guatemala, Peru, Mexico, and Mauritania. Our teachers celebrate our diversity. We are all so different, but we find ways in which we are the same.

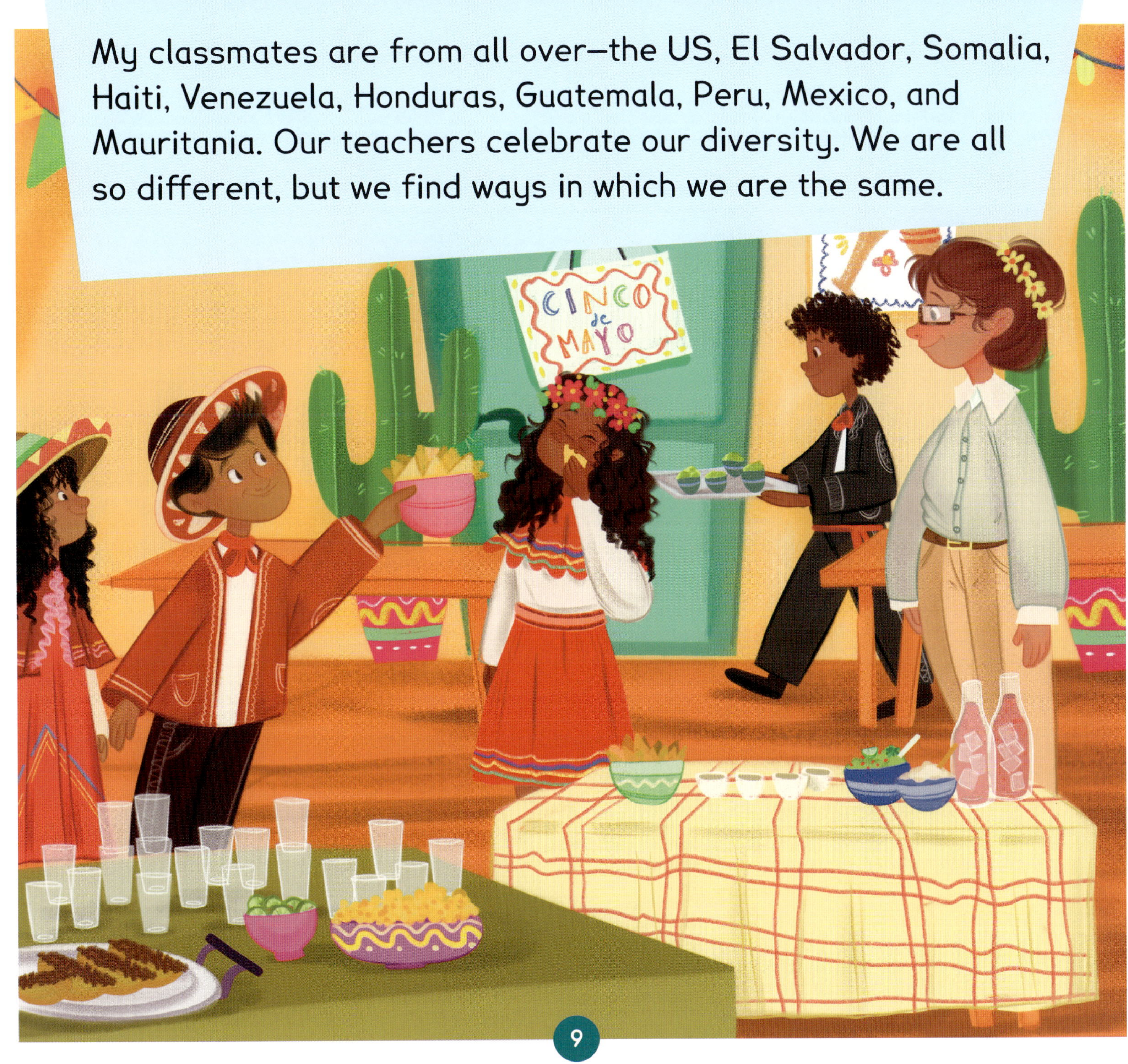

The first friend I made here was Sophia. She is from Honduras. We both have always loved stories. Now, we like to read adventure books side by side.

I'm lucky to have my cousin Andrea in my school, too. We remember different things about El Salvador. It's fun to share our memories about when we were little.

In El Salvador, it was hard for people to find work. In Ohio, my mom and her brothers paint houses. They make homes beautiful, including mine.

Tia Bea, my Aunt Beatrice, is a beautician. She makes people beautiful. We go to her to have our nails done as a special treat.

I was born in a city called Metapán. Evelyn and I would make rock towers in the beautiful river. The city I live in now has a big green park that reminds me of El Salvador.

In Central America, people love football. It's called soccer here. Our favorite team is the Columbus Crew. We cheer them on at home and at games.

When I miss El Salvador, eating home-cooked food comforts me. My whole family gets together for cookouts. We eat pupusas, tacos, and mango with tajin. Yum! Since moving to the US, I have other favorite foods, too. I like burgers, pizza, and ice cream.

It's hard for immigrants when their whole family isn't together. Most of my family is in the US now. Papachico, my great-grandfather, still lives in El Salvador. He is 99, so he can't travel anymore. I text with him, though, and I see his smiling face every week.

There are hard things and good things about being an immigrant. I miss the warm weather, the rock towers, and Papachico in El Salvador. But I love being in the US with my school, my friends, and my cousins.

Immigrants get to keep memories of where they were born and make new ones in their new country. I'm so lucky I get to do both.

Meet Paola

Hi! I'm Paola. I live in Ohio with my mom, stepdad, sister, two brothers, and a cat named Lilo. I was born in El Salvador and moved to the United States when I was five. I love to play soccer and volleyball, and I play violin. In my quiet time, I read books and play video games. When I grow up, I want to be an artist or a professional soccer player.

Welcoming and Respecting Immigrants

A person who moves to a new country might feel scared and lonely. You can help by offering friendship, kindness, and support.

Show a new kid how things work in the lunchroom and invite them to sit with you. At recess, you could invite them to play and introduce them to other students.

An immigrant may not speak much English, so be patient. If they are learning the language, find a game or sport to play that doesn't focus on words.

When you get to know them a bit, ask them about their home country. You can learn about things like the foods they eat, their holidays, and their traditions.

You can share your traditions, too. Maybe your school has a pajama day every year. Let the person know what others have worn, so they know what to expect.

Learn a few words or phrases in the person's native language. It's an easy way to make someone feel comfortable.

Immigrants want to feel welcome, just like everyone else does. Help make that happen by being a warm and welcoming friend!

Helpful Terms

Central America The seven countries south of Mexico and the United States: Belize, Costa Rica, El Salvador, Guatemala, Honduras, Nicaragua, and Panama.

diversity Being made up of different elements, including people from various races, religions, backgrounds, beliefs, and cultures.

great-grandfather The father of one's grandparent.

pupusa A corn or flour pancake stuffed with cheese, meat, or beans and served with slaw and tomato salsa. Pupusa was invented in El Salvador and is the national dish.

reunite To come back together after being separated.

tajin A seasoning made of chili peppers, lime, and sea salt.

Read More

Cords, Sarah. ***Your Passport to El Salvador.*** North Mankato, Minn.: Capstone Press, 2021.

Fernandez, Carolina. ***We Are Immigrants.*** Philadelphia: Running Press Kids, 2024.

Khiani, Darshana. ***I'm an American.*** New York: Viking, 2023.

Thermes, Jennifer. ***A Place Called America: A Story of the Land and People.*** New York: Abrams Books for Young Readers, 2023.

Websites

BRITANNICA KIDS | IMMIGRATION

https://kids.britannica.com/kids/article/immigration/399508

Read a brief history of immigration to the United States.

EL SALVADOR COUNTRY PROFILE—NATIONAL GEOGRAPHIC KIDS

https://kids.nationalgeographic.com/geography/countries/article/el-salvador

Learn about the geography, people, and culture of El Salvador.